BENEDICTIONS

ROBERT I. VASHOLZ

BENEDICTIONS

A Pocket Resource

ROBERT I. VASHOLZ

Robert Vasholz was Chairman of the Old Testament Department at Covenant Theological Seminary, St Louis, Missouri for over twenty-five years. He completed his doctoral studies at the University of Stellenbosch in South Africa. His dissertation compared the Aramaic in Daniel and Ezra with 38 fragments of a Targum of Job uncovered among the Dead Sea Scrolls. He holds a degree from Covenant Theological Seminary and has enjoyed post-doctoral studies at Brandeis and Harvard. He has also written *The Old Testament Canon in the Old Testament Church* which has been reproduced in several languages. He is a native of Kansas City, Missouri. He and his wife, Julia, have one daughter and 5 grandchildren.

Abbreviations

TH   *Trinity Hymnal* Revised Edition, Fifth Printing, 1995. Great Commission Publications, Atlanta, Philadelphia

NASB   Scripture quotations taken from the New American Standard Bible® Copyright © 1960, 1962, 1963, 1968, 1971, 1972, 1973, 1975, 1977, 1995 by The Lockman Foundation Used by permission.

10 9 8 7 6 5 4 3 2 1

ISBN 1-84550-230-2
ISBN 978-1-84550-230-0

Published in 2007
by
Christian Focus Publications,
Geanies House, Fearn, Tain, Ross-shire,
IV20 1TW, Scotland, UK

www.christianfocus.com

Cover design by Danie Van Straaten

Printed and bound by Bercker, Germany

The word benediction derives from two Latin words that mean 'to speak well of'. Benedictions are pronounced by ministers at the close of worship services as an express- ion of hope and encouragement to God's people to face whatever their future might hold. They are a reminder of a good and great God, Who is rich in mercy, Who is not only for them but with them in whatever trials may befall their course in life. It has been my experience, that God's people look earnestly and intently for a final word of divine well-wishing from God through His ministers.

The motivation for this work rose from the general practice by ministers of using only three or four of the same benedictions all the time. While these three or four are superb, it occurred to me that the Scriptures are replete in their well wishing for a divine blessing for the people of God. Once I began to realize this, it seems that almost everywhere I read in Scripture, both in the Old and New Testaments, a hope of blessing for the flock of God appears. What follows then is a number of them for the minister to make the most of, to offer not only a welcomed variety, but for the sake of enhancing the beauty of God's blessings. But it is not only the Scriptures that proffer so much in this regard, but Scripture truth enhanced by poetic expression in so many of our beloved hymns. For this reason, I have included not only benedictions residing in the Scriptures only (1–53), but benedictions as well that combine Scripture with some of the beautiful phraseology found in cherished hymns (54–109).

I am grateful for my colleague, friend and esteemed church historian David B. Calhoun for contributing a brief history of the benediction. We were both surprised at how very little has been written on this topic. Surprised, because it has been a part of worship for so many generations. Indeed, it has its roots in the oldest part of the Old Testament. Numbers 6:24-27, 'The LORD bless you and keep you; the LORD make his face shine upon you and be gracious to you; the LORD turn his face toward you and give you peace. So they will put my name on the Israelites, and I will bless them.'

Robert I. Vasholz

John Calvin's *Form of Church Prayers* for Geneva (1542) directs that the Aaronic 'blessing' of Numbers 6:24-26 be spoken by the minister 'at the departure of the people, according to our Lord's appointment.' The rubric grounds the liturgical practice in the example of Christ at his ascension, when 'he led [the disciples] out as far as Bethany, and lifting up his hands he blessed them' (Luke 24:50). Luther suggested that it was the benediction of Numbers 6:24-26 (or 'something of this kind') that Jesus used on that occasion:

> The Lord bless you and keep you.
> The Lord make his face to shine upon you and be gracious unto you.
> The Lord lift up his countenance upon you and give you peace.

The Reformers found in the Aaronic benediction a profound statement of what the blessing of God means: the promise of grace and peace and the light of God's countenance shining upon his people.

Benedictions, such as the one in Numbers 6, were used in the worship of the synagogue. The central prayer of the synagogue was the *Amida* or the Prayer of Eighteen Benedictions. Each of the petitions and intercessions of the *Amida* ends with a benediction or thanksgiving. For example, the sixth benediction is a prayer for forgiveness: 'Forgive us, our Father, for we have sinned; pardon us, our King, for we have transgressed, for thou art good and forgiving.' This prayer concludes with a sentence that, properly speaking, is the benediction: 'Blessed be thou, O God, who art gracious and dost abundantly forgive.' The synagogue liturgy ended with the Aaronic benediction of Numbers 6.

The prayers of the early church bear the marks of the liturgical mold of the synagogue. The Epistle of Clement, written in Rome at the end of the first century, includes a long prayer with similarities to the *Amida* or Synagogue Prayer. Clement's prayer, which probably reflects the features of the public prayers of the church in Rome at that time, ends with an elaborate benediction:

> Now may God, the all-seeing, and the master of spirits, and the Lord of all flesh, who chose the Lord Jesus Christ, and us through him for 'a peculiar people,' give unto every soul that is called after his glorious and holy name, faith, fear, peace, patience and long suffering, self-control, purity, sobriety, that they may be well pleasing to his name through our high priest and guardian, Jesus Christ, through whom be to him glory and majesty, might and honour, both now and to all eternity. Amen.

Benedictions or blessings served various purposes in the later Catholic church. There were benedictions, or 'sacramentals,' as they were called, for the blessing of persons (at ordinations and installations), things (churches, houses, fields, and even animals), and materials used in worship (oil, candles, baptismal water, and wedding rings). These benedictions were connected with exorcisms – the latter breaking demonic influence and the former cleansing and blessing by divine power. It was believed that the power to bless resided in the church and in the minister giving the benediction.

The Reformers objected to these ideas and practices. Only persons, not things, are to be blessed with God's Spirit and grace. And it is only God who effectively blesses; all human blessing is intercession with God for his blessing.

Johann Gerhard, seventeenth-century Lutheran theologian, explained:

> The [Old Testament] priests blessed by praying for good things; God blessed by bestowing the good things. Their blessing was votive, his effective. God promises to confirm this sacerdotal blessing on condition that it is given according to his word and will.

The Reformers noted that the benedictions of the Bible were more than the traditional way of parting; they were prayers of intercession. Furthermore, they were prayers of intercession by a messenger (such as Aaron, Melchizedek, Balaam, and Simeon) sent by God to proclaim that God had indeed granted the blessing promised in the benediction. The benediction was more than a general prayer of intercession; it was concerned with that spiritual blessing that God gave to Abraham and to his seed forever. That blessing was handed down from generation to generation in the temple and, later, in the church. In Christ Jesus 'the blessing of Abraham' had come to the Gentiles, wrote Paul in Galatians 3:14. Calvin explained that the benediction is God's word in a special sense; it is a proclamation of grace, spoken by God's ministers, by the power of God's Spirit, and received by the people by faith. More than a prayer, it is a sermon. According to Calvin, the blessing God gives is himself.

'By the time of the Reformation,' writes Hughes Oliphant Old, 'the restored benediction [at the end of the service] became an obvious feature of Protestant worship.' Luther's *German Mass* (1526) concludes with the words 'God's Spirit and grace be with us all.' After the sermon in Zwingli's *Zurich Liturgy* (1525) is the prayer 'Almighty, eternal God! Forgive us our sin and lead us to everlasting life, through Jesus Christ our Lord.' Concluding Zwingli's service of the Lord's Supper are the words 'We give thee thanks, O Lord, for all thy gifts and blessings: thou who livest and reignest, God for ever and ever.' Martin Bucer's *Strassburg Liturgy* (1539) ends with the Aaronic benediction followed by the words 'Depart! The Spirit of the Lord go with you unto eternal life!' As noted above, Calvin's *Form of Church Prayers* (1542) concludes with the benediction of Numbers 6:24-26. *The Book of Common Prayer* (1552) directs that the priest or bishop dismiss the people with the words 'The peace of God, which passeth all understanding, keep your hearts and minds in the knowledge and love of God, and of his Son, Jesus Christ our Lord; and the blessing of God

Almighty, the Father, the Son, and the Holy Ghost, be among you, and remain with you always.' John Knox's *Form of Prayers* (1556) instructs the minister to end the service with the benediction of Numbers 6:24-26 or 2 Corinthians 13:14 ('The grace of our Lord Jesus Christ, the love of God, and the communion of the Holy Ghost, be with you all'). *The Middleburg Liturgy* of the English Puritans (1586) follows Knox's liturgy at this point. *The Westminster Directory* (1644) instructs the minister to dismiss the congregation 'with a solemn blessing,' but does not give any specific examples. Richard Baxter's *Savoy Liturgy* (1661) concludes 'with this, or the like,' blessing: 'Now the God of peace, which brought again from the dead our Lord Jesus Christ, that great Shepherd of the sheep, through the blood of the everlasting covenant, make you perfect in every good work to do his will, working in you that which is well pleasing in his sight, through Jesus Christ; to whom be glory for ever and ever.' John Wesley's *Sunday Service of the Methodists in North America* (1784) has the elder using these words to end the service: 'May the God of peace, which passeth all understanding, keep your hearts and minds in the knowledge and love of God and of his Son, Jesus Christ our Lord; and the blessing of God Almighty, the Father, the Son, and the Holy Ghost, be amongst you and remain with you always.'

Many of the Reformation liturgies and those of Irish and Scottish Presbyterianism preserved the dismissal at the conclusion of worship services. In his book *O Come, Let Us Worship*, Robert G. Rayburn taught that 'a few words of dismissal reminding the people of the challenge to serve Christ and to live for Him in this dark world of sin are of real value. ... Such a word as "Go in peace and serve the living God in a world of strife and turmoil" will remind each listener that his worship of God should have prepared for him a richer experience of witnessing for God in the everyday world.' The words of dismissal are followed by the benediction, Rayburn states, for the people should not be sent forth to serve in their own strength. He explains that 'they must ever be dismissed in the name of the Lord with the assurance of the power and presence of the Triune God to accompany them always.'

The gesture that accompanied the benediction in Reformed services was not the sign of the cross, as in Catholicism, but the lifting up of his hands by the minister. It is a gesture of reception, a symbol of God's mercies coming down upon the congregation. The minister receives and passes on to the people the blessing of the presence of God and the peace that God gives. Terry Johnson writes: 'There is considerable disagreement as to the nature of the benediction. Is it a pronouncement, spoken to the congregation with head uplifted and eyes opened, or is it a prayer, prayed with head bowed and eyes closed? ... In either case, arms should be uplifted as the blessing of God is called down from heaven.'

There are many benedictions in the Scriptures. Rayburn insisted that 'a minister should not make up his own when the inspiration of the Holy Spirit has made available ample words of benediction so that there need be no repetitive use of the same one or two.'

In this book Robert Vasholz has collected many of the Bible's benedictions and constructed other scripture-enriched blessings for the use of ministers who lead worship. Indeed all Christians will be 'blessed' by reading and praying these wonderful words from God, such as:

The Lord bless you and keep you.
The Lord make his face to shine upon you and be gracious unto you.
The Lord lift up his countenance upon you and give you peace.

David B Calhoun
Professor of Church History,
Covenant Theological Seminary, St Louis, Missouri

May the One who makes the crocus burst into
   bloom,
Who makes the lame leap like a deer
And the mute tongue shout for joy

Grant you the power together with all of the saints,
to grasp how wide and long and high and deep is the
love of Christ that surpasses all knowledge.

Scripture References

Isaiah 35:1, 6

Ephesians 3:18, 19

May the feeblest among you be like David,
May the God who gives encouragement and endurance,
Give you the Spirit of unity as you follow Christ,
So that with one heart and one mouth we may
    together,
Glorify the God and Father of our Lord Jesus
    Christ.

Scripture References

Zechariah 12:8

Romans 15:5, 6

May the God who shouted, Moab is my washbasin,
Upon Edom I toss my sandal,
Over Philistia I shout in triumph.

Lead you to always triumph in Christ
And spread through you everywhere,
The fragrance of the knowledge of Him.

Scripture References

Psalm 60:8

2 Corinthians 2:14

004 BENEDICTION

May your eyes see the king in his beauty
That you might view a land that stretches afar;
Like Abraham, who looked to a city,
Whose architect and builder is God.

Scripture References

Isaiah 33:17

Hebrews 11:10

And now to God's elect,
Whom He has upheld since they were conceived,
Carried since they were born,

Hear His good promise;
I am he; I will sustain you,
I will carry you,
I will rescue even to your old age.

Scripture Reference

Isaiah 46:3-4

May the Lord guide you always;
May you be like a well-watered garden,
Like a spring whose waters never fail.
When you cry for help, may the Lord always say,
'Here am I'

Scripture Reference

Isaiah 58:9, 11

Now to you from Him Who is, and Who was, and Who is to come ... from Jesus Christ, Who is the faithful witness, the firstborn from the dead and the ruler of the kings of the earth,

May Grace and Peace abound.

Scripture Reference

Revelation 1:4, 5

008 BENEDICTION

Here the word of the Lord,
In favor I will show you compassion,
So that men may bring you the wealth of nations,
In favor I will enlighten the eyes of your heart,

That you might fully understand the hope to which
He called you, even the glorious inheritance of the
saints.

Scripture References

Isaiah 61:6

Ephesians 1:18

May our God who called Abraham when he was but
    one,
And blessed him and made him many,

Show you the incomparable riches of his grace,
That you might know you are His workmanship,
To do good works, which God has prepared in
    advance for us to do.

Scripture References

Isaiah 51:2

Ephesians 2:7, 10

And now may He grace you with his presence,
So that the weak might say, 'I am strong',
And the poor will say, 'I am rich',
And the feeble will say, 'I am upheld'.

Scripture References

Joel 3:10

Isaiah 35:3

2 Corinthians 6:10

May he who builds his lofty palace in the heavens
And sets its foundation on the earth,
Who calls for the waters of the sea
And pours them out over the face of the land

Grant you an awareness of His love that you may
be always joyful, praying continually and giving thanks
in all circumstances
    For this is the will of God for you.

Scripture References

Amos 9:6

I Thessalonians 5:16-18

012 BENEDICTION

Now may God grant you such that you may say like
the psalmist,
You are my hiding place; you protect me from all
trouble
And surround me with songs of deliverance.
So that your work is produced by faith,
Your labor is prompted by love,
and your endurance is inspired by hope in our Lord
Jesus Christ.

Scripture References

Psalm 32:7

I Thessalonians 1:3

May the Lord grant you to see where you are lacking, that you might have everything; May He grant you a vision of your poverty, that you might be rich beyond measure, May He show you that you are destitute so that you may be filled with fullness of His supply.

Scripture Reference

Philippians 3:8

014 BENEDICTION

And now may your experience be like the psalmist who said, 'Surely God is my help, the Lord is the One who sustains me';

May your confidence be as the apostle who said, 'The One who calls you is faithfull, He will do it'.

Scripture References

Psalm 54:4

1 Thessalonians 5:24

May the Lord show kindness to you;
May the Lord grant each of you rest;
May those who dwell in your house be blessed; may
    they ever be praising the Lord.

Scripture References

Ruth 1:8, 9

Psalm 84:4

016 BENEDICTION

May the Lord who has never failed in any of His
   good promises,
Who does not leave or forsake His own,
May He turn your hearts to Him,
To walk in His Ways
And to keep His commands that he gave our fathers
   in the Faith.

Scripture Reference

1 Kings 8:56- 58

Let those who trust the Lord be like Mount Zion,
Which cannot be shaken but endures forever.

May that same Lord establish you in the Gospel
So that all peoples might believe and obey Him
Who is the only wise God; the glory is to Him
forever through Jesus Christ! Amen.

Scripture References

Psalm 125:1

Romans 16:25-27

May the Lord send you help from His sanctuary
And grant you support from on High,
May grace and peace be to you from the God
Who gave himself for our sins to rescue us from the
present evil age.

Scripture References

Psalm 20:2

Galatians 1:3

May you be blessed whose strength is in the Lord
You who have set your hearts in pilgrimage,
Who go from strength to strength,
Til you appear before God in the heavenly Zion.

Scripture Reference

Psalm 84:5, 7

May the Lord establish you as a holy people to
Himself,
May He hover over you as an eagle over its young,
Who spreads its wings and catches them and carries
them on its pinions
To the end that you who have put your hope in
Christ Jesus would be to the praise of His glory.

Scripture References

Deuteronomy 32:11

Ephesians 1:12

Now, as you depart, Take His Yoke upon you and learn from Him for He is gentle and humble of heart that you might find in Him, rest for your souls.

For he has said, I give My sheep eternal life and they shall never perish; no one can snatch them out of My hand.

Scripture References

Matthew 11:28-30

John 10:28, 29

May the same God who delivered David from the paw of the lion, the paw of the bear and the hand of the Philistine, deliver you from our common enemy

So that you will have nothing to do with the fruitless deeds of darkness but rather know that the Lord will reward everyone for whatever good he or she does.

Scripture References

1 Samuel 17:37

Ephesians 5:11; 6:8

May goodness and loving kindness follow you all the
days of your life,
May His loving-kindness and truth continually
preserve you,
So that you can say, the Lord is my shepherd; I shall
not want.

Scripture References

Psalm 23:6; 40:11; 23:1

024 BENEDICTION

May the Father who bought you,
The Father who has made you and established you,
Make you complete, like-minded and comforted
By the God of love and peace..

Scripture References

Deuteronomy 32:6

2 Corinthians 13:11

Philippians 2:2

May your days be like a day the Lord inscribes on the cooking pots in the Lord's House, HOLINESS TO THE LORD.

As God Himself sanctifies you completely so that your spirit, soul and body be preserved without blame until the coming of our Lord Jesus Christ.

Scripture References

Zechariah 14:20, 21

I Thessalonians 5:23

The Lord bless you and keep you;

The Lord make His face shine upon you and be gracious to you;

The Lord lift up His countenance upon you and give you peace.

Scripture Reference

Numbers 6:24-26

May your prayers be counted as incense;
The lifting up of your praise as the evening offering.
Always giving thanks for all things in the name of our
Lord Jesus Christ, to God, even the Father.

Scripture References

Psalm 141:2

Ephesians 5:20

028 BENEDICTION

And to the sheep who hear His voice
    even those the Lord calls by their name.
Know that the Lord is God; It is He who made us
    and we are His.
We are His people, the sheep of His pasture.

Scripture References

John 10:3

Psalm 100:3

Grace and Peace to you who were dead in your sins and in the uncircumcision of your sinful nature, who God made alive in Christ and forgave all of your sins,

Go rejoicing in the Lord and be glad; for you are the upright in heart.

Scripture References

Colossians 2:13, 14

Psalm 32:11

Therefore, since you have received a kingdom, which cannot be shaken by the Lord who said, 'My cities will again over flow with prosperity, the Lord will again comfort Zion and choose Jerusalem'.

May the same Lord fill you with gratitude by which you may offer service acceptable with reverence and awe.

Scripture References

Hebrews 12:28

Zechariah 1:17

May the God who wipes out your transgressions,
    for His sake,
And will not remember your sins,
Continually set you free from the burdens common
    to men,
That you might praise His name.

And that the righteous may gather around the Lord,
Who has dealt bountifully with You.

Scripture References

Isaiah 43:25

Psalm 73:5; 142:7

032 BENEDICTION

Let the beloved of the Lord rest secure in Him,
Let Him shield them all day long,
Let the one the Lord loves rest between His
  shoulders.
That you might be steadfast, immovable and knowing
That your toil in the Lord is not in vain.

Scripture References

Deuteronomy 33:12

I Corinthians 15:58

And now forgetting what is behind, reach forward
    to that what is ahead,
That you may exclaim with the psalmist, I will give
    thanks to Your name,
For Your loving kindness and Your truth,
I will give You thanks with all my heart.

Scripture References

Philippians 3:13

Psalm 138:1, 2

---

034 BENEDICTION

May the Lord of Hosts be with you
So that you will become greater and greater still,
Until you receive that crown of life
Which the Lord has prepared for those that love
Him.

Scripture References

2 Samuel 5:10 (NASB)

James 1:12

May our Lord who saved the great king of Judah,
    Hezekiah,
And the inhabitants of Jerusalem from the King of
    Assyria,
And from the hand of all others,
Enable you to say with confidence,
    The LORD is with me; He is my helper.
    I will look in triumph over my enemies.

Scripture References

2 Chronicles 32:22

Psalm 118:7

May the God who works wonders,
Who has made His strength known among His
  people,
And by His power redeemed them,
May He be your joy and delight in you always

Scripture References

Psalm 77:14, 15

Luke 1:14

Now may He who is the mystery of godliness, He who appeared in a body, was vindicated by the Spirit, was seen by angels, was preached among the nations, was believed on in the world, and taken up in glory; May He humble you under His mighty hand that He may lift you up in due time.

Scripture References

1 Timothy 3:16

1 Peter 5:6

038 BENEDICTION

Now to you who have died, been buried and have
    been raised in Christ,
And whose life has been hidden in Christ and who
    will be revealed with Him in glory;
Go, knowing that it is by your faith that you stand
    firm,
By His life that is at work in you.

Scripture References

Colossians 3:1-4

2 Corinthians 1:24; 4:12

May He Who rides a white horse, Who is called
Faithful and True.

Whose Eyes are like a blazing fire, and upon his head
are many crowns.

Who is dressed in a robe dipped in blood, and
Whose name is the Word of God.

Keep your hearts and your minds in Christ Jesus with
the peace of God that transcends all understanding.

Scripture References

Revelation 19:11-13

Philippians 4:7

Now may He who has rescued us from the domain of darkness, and transferred us to the kingdom of His beloved Son,

Fill you with all knowledge so that you will walk in a manner worthy of the Lord, to please Him in all respects, bearing fruit in every good work, increasing in the knowledge of God.

Scripture References

Colossians 1:13; 1:9, 10

Dear friends, be on your guard so that you may not be carried away by the error of lawless men and fall from your secure position. But grow in the grace and knowledge of our Lord and Savior Jesus Christ. To him is glory both now and forever! Amen.

Scripture Reference

2 Peter 3:17, 18

May your strength in the LORD be like that of king
    Abijah,
Who subdued the enemies of the LORD when he
    and the sons of Judah trusted in the LORD,
the God of their fathers.

Scripture Reference

2 Chronicles 13:18

May the Lord,
Who longs to be gracious to you,
Who waits on high to have compassion on you,
Plant you firmly in the faith, established, steadfast
and unmovable'
Through the hope of the Gospel, proclaimed to all
the creation under heaven.

Scripture References

Isaiah 30:18

Colossians 1:23

Now to you who were formerly alienated and hostile in your mind,

Who have now been reconciled through His death in order to present you holy and blameless and beyond reproach,

Go out in joy and be led forth in peace; until, as it were, the mountains burst into song before you, and all the trees of the field clap their hands.

Scripture References

Colossians 1:21, 22

Isaiah 55:12

And now hear from the God Who dwells in the
heavenly Zion:

Blessed is the one Who He chooses to dwell in His
courts,

For He will satisfy your house with goodness and by
awesome deeds,

Answer all who trust in Him.

Scripture Reference

Psalm 65:4

Now in the name of the One who has made us debt
    free,
And removed that hostility between God and His
    people,
Having removed all of our transgressions.
May He be your confidence and deliver your foot
    from every snare.

Scripture References

Colossians 2:14, 15

Proverbs 3:26

May that One, in whom we have redemption through
   His blood,
The forgiveness of sins, in accordance with the
   riches of His grace,
Lavish on you all wisdom and understanding.
So that you might keep your heart on the right path.
   Amen.

Scripture References

Ephesians 1:7-8

Proverbs 23:19

048 BENEDICTION

Now may the Lord remember us and bless us; for He blesses all those who fear the Lord – both small and great alike.

Scripture Reference

Psalm 115:12-13

And now O Lord, rain down righteousness; let the clouds shower it down. Let the earth open wide, let salvation spring up, let righteousness grow with it;

So that your people may be mature and complete, never lacking anything.

Scripture References

Isaiah 45:8

James 1:4

050 BENEDICTION

May our Lord who has laid up for you a hope in heaven where moth and rust cannot destroy,

Keep you strong to the end, so that you will be blameless on the day of our Lord Jesus Christ.

Scripture References

Colossians 1:5

Matthew 6:19, 20

1 Corinthians 1:8

May the God of hope fill you with all joy and peace in believing, so that by the power of the Holy Spirit you may abound in hope.

Scripture Reference

Romans 15:13

Peace be to you and love with faith from God the Father and the Lord Jesus Christ. Grace be with all who love our Lord Jesus Christ with love incorruptible.

Scripture Reference

Ephesians 6:23, 24

May the Lord answer you in the day of trouble! May the name of the God of Jacob protect you. May you shout for joy over your salvation and may you in the name of our God establish our banners.

Scripture Reference

Psalm 20:1, 5

054 BENEDICTION

Now may He who raises the poor from the dust,
The needy from the ash heap;
And makes them sit with nobles
And inherit a seat of honor.

Bear you through troubled days,
To you who trust in God's unchanging love.

Scripture Reference

1 Samuel 2:8

Hymn Reference

If Thou but Suffer God Guide Thee, Georg Neumark (1621-1681); TH p. 670

To you who are debtors to mercy alone
And free from the terrors of the law.

Walk in the light, as he is in the light, so that the blood of Jesus, God's Son, purifies you from all sin.

Scripture Reference

1 John 1:7

Hymn Reference

A Debtor of Mercy Alone, Augustus Toplady (1740-1778); TH p. 463

056 BENEDICTION

May the bliss of this glorious thought – my sin, not in part but the whole is nailed to the Cross and you bear it no more,

Comfort you in all your troubles so that you may comfort those in trouble with that comfort you have received from God!

Scripture Reference

2 Corinthians 1:4

Hymn Reference

It is Well with My Soul, Horatio G, Spafford (1828-1888); TH p. 691

Go equipped by His Grace,
Surrounded by Salvation's Walls.
Let nothing shake your sure repose,
For no man has laid such a firm foundation,
Other than the One, which is laid, which is Christ
　　Jesus the Lord.

Scripture Reference

I Corinthians 3:11

Hymn Reference

Glorious Things of Thee are Spoken, John Newton (1725-1807); TH p. 345

058 BENEDICTION

May the Great Creator whose power is displayed day by day by an unwearied sun,

Create in you a pure heart and renew in you a steadfast spirit.

Scripture Reference

Psalm 51:10

Hymn Reference

The Spacious Firmament on High, Joseph Addison (1672-1719); TH p. 117

The God who sent His Son to save,
From guilt and darkness and the grave,
be gracious to you and bless you
And cause His face to shine upon you.

Scripture Reference

Psalm 67:1

Hymn Reference

Give to God Our Immortal Praise, Isaac Watts (1674-1748); TH p. 3

060 BENEDICTION

From the God Most High,
Whose ways are mercy and truth,
Who leads you to his heavenly throne.

May He preserve your life according to His
    promise;
Keep you from all harm,
And watch over your life.

Scripture Reference

Psalm 119:107; 121:7

Hymn Reference

Give to God Our Immortal Praise, Isaac Watts (1674-1748); TH p. 3

May our God who has sworn by Himself
Upon whose oath you may depend
Who bears His own on eagle's wind;

May He strengthen you and help you,
May He uphold you with His righteous hand.

Scripture Reference

Isaiah 41:10

Hymn Reference

The God of Abraham Praise, Thomas Olivers (1725-1799); TH p. 34

062 BENEDICTION

Now to you who dwell securely under the shadow
of God's throne,
And who know the sufficiency of God's arm,
May you be active in sharing your faith, so that you
have a full understanding of every good thing we
have in Christ.

Scripture Reference

Philemon 6

Hymn Reference

Our God Our Help in Ages Past, Isaac Watts (1674-1748); TH p. 30

To you whose life is hid with Christ on High,
Whoever lives and pleas for you;
May He keep you from stumbling,
And make you to stand in the presence of His
   glory,
Blameless and with great joy.

Scripture Reference

Jude 24

064 BENEDICTION

May He Who breaks the power of canceled sin and
    sets the prisoner free,
Whose blood can make the foulest clean;

May he increase your understanding so that you
    may know Him who is true,
And that you are in His Son, Jesus Christ.

Scripture Reference

1 John 5:20

Hymn Reference

O for a Thousand Tongues to Sing, Charles Wesley(1707-1788); TH p. 164

And now, press on to maturity,
With the confidence that what're God ordains is
    right,
And though dark may be the road,
He holds you that you shall not fall.

Scripture Reference

Hebrews 6:1

Hymn Reference

Whate'er My God Ordains is Right, Samuel Rodigast (1649-1708); TH p. 108

066 BENEDICTION

And now may Christ,
Who is adored in the highest heaven,
The everlasting Lord,
   the Prince of Peace and Sun of Righteousness,

Fill you with the knowledge of his will through all
   spiritual wisdom and understanding.

Scripture Reference

Colossians 1:9

Hymn Reference

Hark! The Herald Angels Sing, Charles Wesley (1707-1788); TH p. 203

May He who is ris'n with healing in His wi;ngs,
Who brings light and life to all,
Who was born that man no more die;

Restore to you the joy of your salvation and sustain
you with a willing spirit. Amen

Scripture Reference

Psalm 51:12

Hymn Reference

Hark! The Herald Angels Sing, Charles Wesley (1707-1788); TH p. 203

May the Mighty One Who has done great things,
And whose mercy goes on from generation to generation,
When life's perils confound you;
May his counsel guide you and beneath his wings protect you,
And may God be with you till we meet again.

Scripture Reference

Luke 1:49, 50

Hymn Reference

God Be with You Till We Meet Again, Jeremiah E. Rankin (1828-1904); TH p. 385

May He who is full of kindness and compassion,
Who is slow to anger, vast in love;
Whose works of love are of surpassing measure
Keep you in the unity of the Spirit through the bond
of peace.

Scripture Reference

Ephesians 4:3

Hymn Reference

God, my King, Thy Might Confessing, Richard Mant (1776-1848); TH p. 5

070 BENEDICTION

May the God who's watchful eye never sleeps;
The God of wonders, power and love;
May He keep your feet from falling,
And make your thanks endless be,
Until the coming of the salvation that is ready to be
    revealed in the last time.

Scripture Reference

1 Peter 1:5

Hymn Reference

All Praise to God Who Reigns Above, Johann J.Schütz (1640-1690); TH p. 4

May the God whose robe is light,
Whose canopy is space,
Whose mercies are tender and firm to the end.

Show you such love so that you will say with the
psalmist,
You are my lamp, O LORD; the LORD turns my darkness into light.

Scripture Reference

2 Samuel 22:29

Hymn Reference

O Worship the King, Robert Grant (1778-1838); TH p. 2

072 BENEDICTION

Now may the Lord who made the heavens, even the highest heavens, and all their starry hosts, the earth and all that is on it, the seas and all that is in them, Who gives life to everything and Who is worshipped by the multitudes of heavenly hosts.

May that Lord by His eternal spirit, by His all-sufficient merit,
Raise you up to his glorious throne.

Scripture Reference

Nehemiah 9:6

Hymn Reference

Come Thou Long Expected Jesus, Charles Wesley (1707-1788); TH p. 196

May the One Who makes the vapors ascend in clouds
from earth's remotest end,
Whose lightings flash at His commands,
Who holds the tempest in His hands.

Keep you from being ineffective and unproductive in
your knowledge of our Lord Jesus Christ.

Scripture Reference

2 Peter 1:8

Hymn Reference

Exalt the Lord, His Praise Proclaim, Franz Joseph Haydn (1732-1809); TH 12

074 BENEDICTION

May He Who has revealed to every nation His everlasting righteousness,
Who sits enthroned in ageless splendor,
Rule in your hearts since as members of one body
you were called to peace.

Scripture Reference

Colossians 3:15

Hymn Reference

New Songs of Celebration Render, Erik Routley (1917-1982); TH p. 14

And now let all men in Zion declare his gracious
name,
With one accord,
So that all nations will fear the name of the LORD,
That a people yet to be created may praise the
LORD.

Scripture Reference

Psalm 102:15, 18

Hymn Reference

The Lord has heard and Answered Prayer, Peter Huford; TH p. 29

May you dwell under the shadow of God's throne,
Where saints have dwelt secure,
Where His arm is sufficient and your defense is sure.

And may you be wise like the conies who, though small, make their houses in the crags of the rocks and are safe from all predators.

Scripture Reference

Proverbs 30:26

Hymn Reference

Our God Our Help in Ages Past, Isaac Watts (1674-1748); TH p. 30

May the Lord your God, our help in ages past,
And our hope for years to come,
Be your guard while troubles last,
And lead you to His eternal throne.

Hymn Reference

Our God Our Help in Ages Past, Isaac Watts (1674-1748); TH p. 30

078 BENEDICTION

May the God Who changes not,
Who has no shadow of turning,
And Whose compassions fail not,
Preserve you by His loving kindness,
So that you might know,
Great are His faithful acts, they are new every morning.

Scripture Reference

Lamentations 3:22, 23

Hymn Reference

Great is Thy Faithfulness, Thomas O. Chisholm (1866-1960); TH p. 32

May the only One Who grants pardon for sin and a
     peace that endures,
And Whose own presence guides and cheers,
Strengthen and protect you from the evil one.

Scripture Reference

2 Thessalonians 3:3

Hymn Reference

Great is Thy Faithfulness, Thomas O. Chisholm (1866-1960); TH p. 32

080 BENEDICTION

May the God of Abraham Who reigns enthroned
    above,
Even the Ancient of everlasting days, the God of love,
Inspire you to behold His face and to make Him
    your shield and high tower.
So that you believe He is and that He is the rewarder
    of those who seek Him.

Scripture Reference

Hebrews 11:6

Hymn Reference

The God of Abraham Praise, Thomas Olivers (1725-1799); TH p. 34

And now, may the only true God -
Immortal, invisible, God only wise,
In light inaccessible hid from our eyes,
Most blessed and glorious, the Ancient of Days,
Be to you glory, majesty, power and authority, through Jesus Christ our Lord, before all ages, now and forevermore! Amen.

Scripture Reference

Jude 25

Hymn Reference

Immortal, Invisible, God only Wise, Walter Chalmers Smith (1824-1908); TH p. 38

082 BENEDICTION

May the God Who is our refuge and our strength,
Our ever-present aid,
The Lord of Hosts who is at our side,
Though the mountains slip into the heart of the sea,
And the earth should change,
May the Lord of Hosts be with you and the God of
Jacob your stronghold.

Scripture Reference

Psalm 46:1, 2

Hymn Reference

God is our Refuge and Our Strength, Goffreid W. Fink (1783-1846); TH p. 40

May the Lord who does not forsake those who earnestly seek His face,
Who provides a safe retreat for weary souls in troubled times.

Show you to be a stronghold for the oppressed,
A stronghold in time of trouble.

Scripture Reference

Psalm 9:9

Hymn Reference

O Lord Most High, with all my Heart, Edward Miller (1735-1807); TH p. 48

May the One who sent His Son with power to save
From guilt, and darkness and the grave,
Whose ways are mercy and truth;

May He never stop doing you good; May He inspire
you to fear Him so that you will never turn aside
from Him.

Scripture Reference

Jeremiah 32:40

Hymn Reference

Give to God Our Immortal Praise, Isaac Watts (1674-1748); TH p. 3

May He who guides our feet through this vain world,
To lead us to His heavenly seat;
Whose mercies shall ever endure,
When this frail world shall be no more.

Help you to contend in the cause of the Gospel with your fellows whose names are written in the Book of Life.

Scripture Reference

Philippians 4:3

Hymn Reference

Give to God Our Immortal Praise, Isaac Watts (1674-1748); TH p. 3

086 BENEDICTION

May the God who did not spare His own Son,
But sent Him to gladly bear our burden on the Cross.

Remind you always of these things, though you know them and are firmly established in the truth, until you arrive to a full measure of glory.

Scripture Reference

2 Peter 1:12

Hymn Reference

How Great Thou Art, Stuart K. Hine; TH p. 44

May the Lord your God be to you a safe retreat
In troubled times, a stronghold and refuge when you
    are oppressed,
So that you can say, I will be glad and rejoice in you,
I will sing praise to your name O Most High.

Scripture Reference

Psalm 9:9, 2

Hymn Reference

O Lord Most High, with all my Heart, Edward Miller (1735-1807); TH p. 48

088 BENEDICTION

May that One whose love has no limit,
Whose grace has no measure,
Whose power has no boundary known unto men.
May He from His infinite riches in Jesus,
Send you help from His sanctuary and grant you His
support from that heavenly Zion.

Scripture Reference

Psalm 20:2

Hymn Reference

'He Giveth More Grace' Annie J. Flint (1866-1932)

May the Lord grant you
The love that leads the way,
The faith that nothing can dismay,
The hope no disappointments can dismay,
And the passion that burns like fire.

Reference

From the biography of Amy Carmichael, p. 327

---

090 BENEDICTION

The God of peace be with you,
Until you see that happy place and be forever blessed,
Until you see your Father's face and in his bosom rest.

Scripture Reference

Romans 15:33

Hymn Reference

On Jordan's Stormy Banks, Samuel Stennet (1727-1795)

May Heaven's richest blessing come down on every-one who goes out, following the good and beautiful Shepherd himself, to find the lost sheep and to love and care for them. For 'beautiful are the feet of those who preach the good news.'

(Gleaned from David Calhoun's chapel talk)

Scripture References

Isaiah 52:7

Romans 10:15

Now may the Son who redeems us,
The Spirit Who renews us,
And the Father Who receives us, for so great is His
    love,
Be gracious to us and bless us and make His face
    shine upon us.

Scripture Reference

Psalm 67:1

Psalm 103.11

May the Lamb upon His throne,
Whose heavenly anthems drown all music than its own;
The Potentate of Time and Creator of the rolling spheres,
Who blesses the righteous;

Surround you like a shield with His favor.

Scripture Reference

Psalm 5:12

Hymn Reference

Crown Him with Many Crowns, Matthew Bridges (1800-1894); TH p. 295

094 BENEDICTION

May the Lord prosper your work and defend you,
May his goodness and mercy attend you,
May you ponder anew what the Almighty will do,
That you may rejoice with all your heart and that
    never again fear any harm,

Scripture Reference

Zephaniah 3:14, 15

Hymn Reference

Praise the Lord, the Amighty, Joachim Neander (1650-1680); TH p. 53

Now may your rising soul survey
The mercies of your God;
May you be lost in wonder, love and praise,
So that through every period of your life
His goodness you will pursue,
Until our Lord Comes again.

Scripture Reference

Revelation 2:25

Hymn Reference

When All Your Mercies, O My God, Joseph Addison (1672-1719); TH p. 56

096 BENEDICTION

May you sing the glorious praises of your God
  through all your days;
May you put no confidence in princes nor for help
  on man depend;
That the Lord who gives strength to the weary and
  increases the power of the weak,
Make you to run and not grow faint, make you to
  walk and not fall.

Scripture Reference

Isaiah 40:29-31

Hymn Reference

Hallelujah Praise Jehovah, Lowell Manson; TH p. 57

Now may the God Who tends and spares us and
    well knows our feeble frame;
Our Father who gently bears us and rescues us
    from our foes,
Establish you like Mt. Zion, which cannot be moved
    but abides forever.

Scripture Reference

Psalm 125:1

Hymn Reference

Praise My Soul the King of Heaven, Henry F. Lyte (1793-1847); TH p. 76

May the Lord be with those who do well.
May He tell you the story of Jesus,
And write on your heart every word,
Till you sing with angels in chorus:
Glory to God in the highest
Peace and good tidings to earth.

Scripture Reference

2 Chronicles 19:11

Hymn Reference

Tell me the Story of Jesus, Fanny J. Crosby(1820-1915); TH p. 234

And now, may the Man of Sorrows
Who came to reclaim ruined sinners,
Who sealed your pardon with His blood,
And made a full atonement for helpless we.

Bless you from Zion all the days of your life,
And direct your hearts into God's love and into the
steadfastness of Christ.

Scripture Reference

2 Thessalonians 3:5

Hymn Reference

Hallelujah! What a Savior, Philip P. Bliss (1838-1876); TH p. 246

---

100 BENEDICTION

May the Lord who never sleeps,
Who Keeps Israel in His holy care,
Who will not suffer that your foot be moved,
Nor fail in his certain aid,

Keep you from now on, yea, forever more.

Scripture Reference

Psalm 121:3, 4

Hymn Reference

Unto the hills around do I lift my longing eyes, John Campbell, Duke of
Argyll (1845-1914); TH p. 96

May the God who ordains that which is right
Though dark the road and sorrow, need, or pain be
    your lot,
Grant you sweet comfort to fill your heart
And be content in what He has sent,
Knowing that His hand can turn your griefs away.

Hymn Reference

Whate'er My God Ordains is Right, Samuel Rodigast (1649-1708); TH p. 108

---

102 BENEDICTION

Now may you be satisfied to fill a little space if God
be glorified,
And not hurry to and fro seeking for some great
thing to do,
But seek from God daily strength while keeping at
His side,
Till you can say with the apostle of old, I have learned
to be content
In whatever circumstance I am in.

Scripture Reference

Philippians 4:11

Hymn Reference

Father I know that all my life, Anna L. Waring (1823-1910); TH p. 559

And now may the God who sought you when a
  stranger, wandering from the fold of God
Who interposed His precious blood to rescue you
  from danger.
Give you voices to praise Him, for to sing His praises
  is good, pleasant and becoming. Amen

Scripture Reference

Psalm 147:1

Hymn Reference

Come Thou Fount of Every Blessing, Robert Robinson (1735-1790); TH p. 457

104 BENEDICTION

Now may our Saviour, Who cheers each winding path we tread, gives grace for every trial and feeds us with His living Bread,

Grant you strength when you are weary,
And increase your power when you are weak.

Scripture Reference

Isaiah 40:29

Hymn References

On Jordan's Stormy Banks, Samuel Stennet (1727-1795)

All the Way My Savior Leads Me, Fanny J. Crosby (1820-1915); TH p. **478**

And now may Jesus, Who satisfies our longings like
nothing else can do
Who is more pleasant than all the fancies of our
golden dreams

May that Lord make your love increase and overflow
for each other and for everyone else.

Scripture Reference

I Thessalonians 3:12

Hymn Reference

I Love to Tell the Story, Arabella Katherine Hankey (1834-1911); TH p. 478

---

106 BENEDICTION

May the One Who takes nobodies and makes them
    somebodies;
Who takes the ridiculous and turns it to the sublime;
Who raises those from the dustbins and crowns
    them princes and princesses;
Cause you to prosper in every good work
And to increase in the knowledge of God.

Scripture References

I Samuel 2:8

Colossians 1:10

May He Who is your light, your strength, your song
   and cornerstone,
Prepare you for the fiercest drought and storm;
Quiet your fears and cease your strivings;
That you may know the heights of His love
And the depths of His peace.

Reference

A benediction after a chapel message by David B. Calhoun

---

108 BENEDICTION

Go, dwell on his love by sweetest song,
And crown His head with multitudes of praises.
Till all kings bow down to him and all nations serve
    Him.

Scripture Reference

Psalm 72:11

Hymn Reference

Jesus Shall Reign, Isaac Watts (1674-1748); TH p.441

May grace, the well-spring of all mercies and peace, the crown of all blessings, be bestowed upon you from God our Father. Amen.

Scripture References

Colossians 1:2

David Short with David Searle

PASTORAL VISITATION
A POCKET MANUAL

Designed for those visiting at home or in hospital

PASTORAL VISITATION:

A Pocket Resource

Designed for those visiting at home or in hospital

David Short with David Searle

Visiting the sick, lonely or downcast is a duty we all have as Christians. It is not to be left to ministers or elders but is a responsibility for all those who seek to follow Christ's perfect example. The prob-lem often arises when we actually make the visit. Discussing the weather or the hospital food is all very well but for our visit to have maximum value we need to try and help the person spiritually. Reading our favourite Bible passage might suffice once but it cannot be apt to every situation and what happens when you visit for a second time?

This is where this book helps. Providing Scripture readings, a prayer and even a suggested hymn for a wide range of possible visits it is a wonderfully useful tool. Written by authors with long pastoral experience it will prove a real help to all those who seek to turn the routine visit into a time of real spiritual growth.

David Short was a Consultant Cardiologist at Aberdeen Royal Infirmary for some 25 years, he was appointed Physician to Her Majesty the Queen in 1977. In addition he was both a preacher of God's Word and a pastor, particularly to the sick, bereaved and discouraged. He died in May 2005.

David Searle was, until his retirement in 2005, Director of Rutherford House, a theological research and study centre in Edinburgh. Prior to that he pastored two Churches of Scotland before moving to Northern Ireland where he pastored Hamilton Road Presbyterian Church for eight years from 1985.

ISBN 1-84550-016-4

KINDLED FIRE

HOW THE METHODS OF **C. H. SPURGEON**
CAN HELP YOUR PREACHING

ZACK ESWINE

'Spurgeon comes alive in these pages!
Zack Eswine has done a masterful job. This
book, like Spurgeon's sermons, feeds the
mind and stirs the heart.'

ALISTAIR BEGG

KINDLED FLAME

Learning to Preach from Charles Haddon Spurgeon

Zack Eswine

'Spurgeon comes alive in these pages! Zack Eswine has done a masterful job. This book, like Spurgeon's sermons, feeds the mind and stirs the heart.'

Alistair Begg, Pastor,
Parkside Community Church, Chagrin Fall, Ohio

'As hard as it may be for 21st century preachers to believe, Charles Spurgeon dealt with many of the same challenges today's preacher's face. Throughout the pages of this fascinating book, the reader feels drawn into Spurgeon's presence and receives valuable counsel as if from the great preacher's own lips. This is a volume that is both enjoyable and rewarding.'

Michael Duduit, Editor,,
Preaching magazine

'In this work Spurgeon lives again not merely as a preacher but as a teacher of preachers for his generation and ours. Eswine honestly explores the strengths and weakness, theology and practice, personality and passions of Spurgeon to guide us on a path toward sound, gracious, and Spirit-empowered preaching for our time.'

Bryan Chapell, President,,
Covenant Theological Seminary, St. Louis, Missouri

Zack Eswine is a Professor of Homiletics at Covenant Theological Seminary, St. Louis, Missouri.

ISBN 1-84550-117-9